GREEK FOOD
FOR SHARING

EUGENIA PANTAHOS

PUBLICATION DETAILS

First published in 2019 by Greek Lifestyle
Author: Eugenia Pantahos

Title: Greek Food For Sharing: Recipes That Nourish The Soul

ISBN: 978-0-9925153-6-2 (Paperback)

Subjects: Cooking, Greek
  Mediterranean Diet
  Greek Food
  International Cuisine
  Cookbooks, Food & Wine,
  Regional & International, Greek

Text copyright © Eugenia Pantahos 2019, Design Cover © Eugenia Pantahos 2019, Photography © Eugenia Pantahos 2019, and Clique Creative 2014, Editing Services Robert Horne, 2019.
Front Cover Design Concept: Steve Grice

The moral right of the author has ben asserted.

All rights reserved. No part of this publication may be reproduced, stored in a retrieval system or transmitted in any form or by any means (electronic, mechanical, photocopying, recording, or otherwise) without the prior written permission of the publisher of this book.

Errors & Omissions Excepted
Copyright © 2019

 A catalogue record for this book is available from the National Library of Australia

COOKING NOTES: Cooking times may vary depending on the oven you are using. 250ml cup used for measurement.

www.greeklifestyle.com.au

GREEK FOOD
FOR SHARING

recipes that nourish the soul

EUGENIA PANTAHOS

www.greeklifestyle.com.au

STYLING AND SLEECTED PHOTOGRAPHY
BY EUGENIA PANTAHOS

PRAISE FOR GREEK LIFE

'A beautiful book which pays homage to timeless Greek traditions. It's easy to get lost in the vivid photographs, and the recipes are simple and a joy to follow. Every Greek family should own this book. Love it!'

'Greek Life is a book that brings the story of family, culture, traditions and recipes all together. I love the introduction and the heartfelt story of Eugenia's family. The book is sprinkled with some very thought-provoking Greek philosophy, authentic recipes, and beautiful yet unique images of Greek food and customs. I've been waiting for a book like this.'

'A truly special book that I'm glad to have found. Greek Life is a real joy and answers some of the questions that I've had. I love the recipes and images. Thank you Eugenia for bringing it all together.'

'Australian-born Eugenia Pantahos dispenses with superficial and sentimental views of Greek cuisine and traditions to embrace a more sophisticated and accurate vision of a complex culture.'

'Every now and then you come across a beautifully presented book that represents everything you've grown up loving. GREEK LIFE is just that! This gorgeous hard-covered book invites you to go on an extraordinary journey of Greek customs, traditions, culture and recipes.'

'Everyone is talking about this book. You should be so proud.'

'I purchased my signed copy yesterday. I just wanted to say your book is an absolute treasure, and beautifully done.'

'This book belongs to us all. We can all relate.'

'Everyone should have a copy of this beautiful book, filled with Greek traditions and culture to be passed on for generations to come!! Gorgeous coffee table book and even better recipe book!! Love it and it sits proudly on mine. Thanks Eugenia!! Great for Greek and non-Greek homes to enjoy.'

For my family, my friends,
and the lovers of Greek culture
and food wherever you are
in the world.

Thank you for joining the celebration.

Eugenia

Contents

014	Introduction
031	Dips
045	Mezze
061	Soups
077	Mains
121	Salads
137	Fruit
143	Coffee
149	Sweets
169	Filo Pastry

INTRODUCTION

Much has happened since the launch of Greek Life. That very first book took on a whole new meaning when a few months after I shared the final draft with my beloved mother, she sadly passed away. Importantly I was given her blessing for the writing of Greek Life, and each copy is infused with that blessing, her love, and her good wishes.

The loss of our matriarch Maria Desyllas, gave a sense of urgency in bringing forth Greek Life as it captured my parents' life, our family history, and timeless authentic recipes. It encapsulated our life in a volume to be treasured by the current and future members of my family.

Throughout the journey of manifesting Greek Life into reality my family stood beside me and encouraged my tireless efforts. I felt very privileged to have Greek Life stocked in some of the best bookstores and gift shops in Australia, and throughout that process I developed meaningful and long lasting relationships.

I spent treasured time with my dear father John Desyllas, in helping him cope with the loss of his beloved Maria; my dear mother. We shared our grief. We sat together with other members of our family, as he talked and we listened. Sometimes we sat in silence remembering and thinking about mum. Sometimes we laughed and sometimes we cried. Sometimes we talked and he listened. But all the time we celebrated the person she was, while missing her dearly.

Over time life became just that little bit easier, as we know, time gently heals grief. Before I knew it the launch of Greek Life was happening. Many gathered to celebrate with me, including my husband and children, my father and extended family, friends, acquaintances. It was a memorable event that happened to be part of a Greek cultural festival in the city in which I live. I clearly remember that evening just like it was yesterday and not quite believing that those attending had showed up to celebrate me as an author and to witness the launch of my book Greek Life. I missed having my mother to share the occasion with, but I knew she was with me in spirit.

Over the next few years I had many public speaking engagements, book talks, interviews for magazines, newspaper, radio and television. I hosted Taste of Greece dinners and travelled interstate for events and promotion of my book.

Many of these occasions were shared with my father and immediate family and that made the journey even more meaningful. But nothing could compare with the feeling I experienced when on multiple occasions my father expressed just how proud he was of me, and how happy he was. I will treasure those memories forever.

Greek Life has been embraced in all corners of the globe and sits proudly in homes for which Greek culture means something. I found this experience humbling and precious all at once, especially as the initial purpose of Greek Life was as a private edition for my immediate and extended family.

From 2016 I spent almost everyday with my father as he faced some health challenges, and in late September 2017, almost a year and half later, he sadly passed away.

Life would never quite be the same. There are no words that I can include here to adequately express the loss of a man who was not only my father, but also a friend and a mentor.

A few weeks later, I received an email advising me that Greek Life won Best Mediterranean Cookbook for Australia in the prestigious Gourmand International Cookbook Awards.

I knew both my parents, in spirit, shared this auspicious occasion with me, as did those around me.

In 2018 I was fortunate to experience extensive travel, with a trip to Montreal in Canada for a wedding and a book signing, a few nights in New York that included having dinner with the national president and select committee members of a Hellenic society, who had previously purchased my book, and with whom I now enjoy friendships.

Next up I travelled to Greece to visit family and friends and to fulfil an invitation to attend an international conference for Hellenes from the diaspora, as well as researching family history and regional foods.

A couple of months later I was once again in Greece to catch up with family and friends as I made my way to the Frankfurt Book Fair in Germany for my book Greek Life. I couldn't have imagined the journey my book would take me on and the wonderful people who came into my life along the way.

The idea for my new cookbook Greek Food For Sharing was forming and I started to type up some of my most favourite recipes, and continued to photograph the food that I prepared in my own kitchen throughout the seasons.

While travelling in Greece and in particular to my parents' birthplace Skourohori, Pyrgos Ilias in the Peleponnese, I continued my writing, and could not resist photographing the food prepared by my family and friends. Some of these photos have been included with my precious recipes, forever uniting our families in a truly beautiful way. After all, we share the same regional cuisine.

When I walked into their kitchens the aromas were identical to that of my late mother's cooking, and the food that I prepare in my own kitchen. I immediately knew that I was about to partake in authentic regional food prepared with love, using only the best homegrown ingredients. I felt so welcome, basking in family love and friendship, lively conversations, passionate story telling whilst savouring each delicious mouthful.

Upon visiting various family and friends I was served a variety of homemade spoon sweets, be it quince, orange, blackcurrant and fig, aromatic and delicious homemade biscuits, and a divine blackcurrant liqueur. The way, in which coffee was prepared and presented on its own tray together with a chilled glass of water and spoon sweet, was a truly elegant experience.

I dined on the most amazing home cooked food, be it a simple rich and thick tomato sauce spooned over perfectly cooked pasta and served with a glass of homemade red wine, or cod fish stew, vegetarian moussaka, lentil soup, perfectly fried fish, plus so many mouth-watering mostly vegetarian and vegan meals. Make no mistake, vegetables and legumes are star attractions in Greek cuisine.

The pride these women have in the food and drinks they prepare using local ingredients, in slow time, made with love and presented with love is an experience to behold. I felt loved, nurtured, included, relaxed, connected and happy.

As I walked through the village naturally people were intrigued, and I found that they were enquiring about my family connections. This is something quite unique to the Greeks, as they are not interested in what you do, instead they want to know where you're from, seeking to learn where the common connection is. The individual person is more important than a job or title.

I loved witnessing the aha moment when people realised who my parents were, and I thoroughly enjoyed the sudden and priceless experience of being swept into an embrace, kissed on both cheeks, patted on the shoulder, having an arm wrapped around mine, or having both hands held by an elder as I listened to animated story telling. I admired their faces full of expression and warmth, carefully taking in each word as they brought my parents to life through their storytelling. My heart felt full of love and nostalgia.

I was bestowed with bundles of homemade biscuits, bunches of black currants, homemade hilopites (square cut pasta), a bottle of liqueur and so much more. These wonderful, generous warm-hearted people spoilt me with expressions of philoxenia. I was blown away, literally, by the love and inclusion shown to me, and the respect and admiration they had for my late parents.

The wonderful moments shared with extended family and friends were enriching, truly memorable, and unforgettable. Collectively these experiences nurtured my spirit, nourished my soul, and deepened the connection to my heritage.

Greece is always a good idea!

When there is love, there is always room at the table.

AN ACT OF LOVE

Nothing is more satisfying and meaningful than family members from across the generations gathered around a table with a colourful assortment of mouth-watering foods made for sharing.

What the Greeks do best is celebrating life with lively conversation, animated story-telling and philosophising over a glass of wine or two – passionately sharing views, laughing and being expressive. Food and drinks are always more enjoyable when shared with family and friends!

In my view, cooking for family and friends is quite simply *an act of love*, from planning the menu, taking into consideration dietary factors and preferences, sourcing only the finest seasonal ingredients.

I choose locally grown and in-season produce, and that means fruits and vegetables are picked at their peak, brimming with higher nutritional value for improved health and wellbeing.

It's a privilege harvesting fresh greens, sun-ripened tomatoes, luscious figs, aromatic fruits, and an assortment of fragrant herbs and citrus from my garden. Cooking with the seasons is something that I simply adore.

As it is in Homer's Odyssey, feasting is a unifying celebration.

FOOD OF MYTHS AND LEGENDS

The Greeks are fascinated with myths and legends. Ambrosial offerings of food and drink reserved for the immortals, those mythical gods and goddesses who sipped on aromatic nectar.

We mere mortals are known to pursue the *Elixir of Life*, and the way we achieve this is to enjoy a vast and colourful assortment of exquisite foods and wines that would please both Epicurus and Dionysius.

Fond of our creature comforts, we anoint our bodies with sweetly scented perfumes and ointments, and surround ourselves with beautiful objects that glitter and shimmer. Our own personal living spaces become sanctuaries where we indulge in scented candles, fresh flowers, spiced teas, and the pursuit of happiness.

What better place to purse the *Elixir of Life* than through the food experiences of Greek cuisine? Harness your inner god or goddess and join me on a divinely gastronomic journey of aromatic deliciousness that can easily be enjoyed by mortals and immortals alike. Celebrate life, family and friendship, and reminisce, rejoice and partake in shared experiences that become tomorrow's memories.

The Greeks are known for their warmth and generosity, and their hospitality is legendary.

MEDITERRANEAN LIFESTYLE

The Greek diet and way of life is part of what I like to call the Mediterranean *lifestyle*. Food is prepared with passion, served with love, and each mouthful is savoured. Lingering over small, shared plates of a colourful assortment of mezedes is an experience like no other, and for the Greeks this is truly an art form.

This particular way of eating means that most nutrients are sourced from whole grain foods, seasonal vegetables, sun-ripened fruits, olive oil, pulses, nuts, seeds, olives, aromatic herbs, seafood, limited dairy and poultry and very limited red meat. Vegetables and legumes are considered star attractions and are not relegated to simple side dishes. The famously popular Greek cuisine is infused with zesty and sun-kissed flavours of the Mediterranean that are not only healthy but enliven the senses.

Since ancient times, Greeks understood the importance of drinking moderate amounts of wine on a daily basis, especially enjoyed with food. I remember my mother, at mealtimes, dipping her last piece of bread into her wine, not wanting to waste a single morsel. There was something sacred in that.

Key factors that make up the highly regarded Mediterranean Lifestyle include incidental physical activity that is usually taken as a daily walk, dancing, gardening, and a relaxed attitude to life.

Socialising and connections to the community are also of great benefit to health and wellbeing and together these factors make up the unique way of living that is espoused by the Greeks.

Recipes that include meat, seafood, poultry, and dairy can easily be modified for vegetarians and vegans, and for times of lent and fasting. These foods become *nistisima* and therein lies the beauty of this uncomplicated way of eating.

The iconic elegance of Greek cuisine is derived from the minimal need for handling ingredients. This classic cuisine is most distinctive with the fragrant and aromatic properties of olive oil, lemon juice and dried oregano. These signature ingredients are used to season vegetables, meats, poultry, seafood and salads.

The flavours of Greece are simple yet sophisticated, be it sun-ripened tomatoes, delightful cucumbers, olives, feta cheese, delicate filo pastries, warm spices, freshly harvested herbs and wild greens, medicinal teas, wine, and of course fruity and aromatic olive oil.

Olive oil is used in both savoury and sweet dishes, and also in religious ceremonies. But nothing compares to the deliciousness and health benefits of enjoying food that has been bathed in what Homer called 'liquid gold'. Dipping a piece of bread into the tangy dressing at the bottom of a bowl of Greek salad is a divine experience.

Honey is the sweetener of choice. It's the nectar of flowers, herbs and trees, in varying hues and flavours. It is enjoyed drizzled over *loukoumades* (donuts), *tiganites* (pancakes), or over natural yoghurt, and as a sweetener for cakes. With its cleansing and antiseptic properties, Greeks use honey at home to soothe a sore throat, as a natural sweetener to an herbal tea, or enjoyed smoothed over fresh bread and butter.

Whether enjoyed at the start of the day, a mid-morning pick-me-up, or after a meal, having a Greek coffee can be quite simply turned into an art form.

This pulverized coffee is prepared in a *briki* and served in demitasse cups along with a glass of water. The sugar is added at the time of making. Hosts will check their guests' preference of either *sketos* (plain, no sugar), *metrio* (medium, 1 sugar) or *glyko* (sweet, 2 sugar), before preparing the coffee in a *briki* over the stove top.

Greek coffee contains higher concentrations of protective antioxidants and polyphenols, and the way in which it is prepared – boiled not filtered – delivers important protective compounds and is believed to boost the overall immune health.

Being a good guest is of equal importance to being a good host. One must always bring them best selves to the table to allow for a meal to be enjoyed with harmony, humour, and happiness.

Every meal is an occasion, and those visiting are always made to feel like a guest of honour. Both the ancient and modern Greeks value *philoxenia*, the art of extending hospitality, generosity, and courtesy to strangers. This is a significant and revered way of life whereby humble strangers are greeted with warmth and inclusion. There is a belief that strangers may be disguised as a deity with the special gift to bestow blessings. Therefore the art of welcoming strangers is a way of not rejecting those gods or goddesses and their blessings.

Greeks love to take time with their food. There is a certain casual elegance and distinctive enjoyment in sitting around a table, sipping on wine and savouring mouthfuls of food prepared as part of the slow food methodology, taking all the time that's needed, for there really is no reason to rush.

Stin iyeia mas!

To our health!

Greek food is known to be fresh, seasonal and incredibly delicious.

The use of herbs, spices and citrus enliven the senses.

DIPS

WHITE BEAN DIP

Ingredients
400gm can cannellini beans, drained and rinsed
1 tablespoon tahini
¼ cup of olive oil
Juice of ½ lemon, or more depending on taste
½ teaspoon cumin
½ small clove of garlic, or to taste
1 tablespoons water, or more if necessary
Salt and pepper

Topping
1 tablespoons sesame seeds, toasted
1 teaspoon finely chopped parsley
¼ teaspoon sweet paprika
Olive oil

Method
In a blender place the cannellini beans, tahini, olive oil, lemon juice, salt, pepper, cumin and garlic. Pulse until the mixture becomes smooth and creamy, adding a little water if necessary. Season to taste with salt and pepper.

Transfer the bean dip to a serving bowl. Drizzle with a little olive oil, sprinkle with sweet paprika, toasted sesame seeds and finely chopped parsley.

Serve with crackers, fresh continental bread or lightly toasted pita bread.

MELIZANOSALATA
AUBERGINE DIP

Ingredients
1 large eggplant, whole and unpeeled
1 small garlic clove, or to taste
¼ cup olive oil
3 tablespoons fresh lemon juice
¾ cup soft fresh white breadcrumbs
2 tablespoons chopped parsley
Salt and pepper

Method
Wash the eggplant, using the tines of a fork pierce the eggplant a few times on either side.

Place the eggplant onto a baking tray lined with baking paper and cook in a moderate oven until the skin is blackened and the flesh is soft to touch.

When ready, carefully remove the skin from the hot eggplant and place the flesh into a blender before adding garlic, lemon juice, breadcrumbs, and parsley.

Pulse until the mixture becomes smooth and creamy, adding a little water if necessary Season to taste with salt and pepper.

Transfer to a serving bowl and drizzle with a little olive oil.

SKORDALIA
GARLIC DIP

Ingredients
1 cup of stale white bread cut into pieces
1 small clove garlic, or to taste
¼ cup of olive oil
3 tablespoons of white vinegar
½ teaspoon salt
White pepper
1-2 tablespoons water or more, if required

Method
Remove crusts from bread and cut roughly into pieces.

Place the bread into an electric blender and add the garlic, olive oil, white vinegar, and salt.

Pulse until the mixture becomes smooth and creamy, adding a little water if necessary.

Make necessary adjustment to the taste to prepare sauce to your liking adding a little more olive oil or vinegar. Season to taste with salt and white pepper.

Transfer to a serving bowl and drizzle with a little olive oil.

KARIDI SKORDALIA
WALNUT DIP

Ingredients
1 potato, cut into cubes, boiled
2 piece of stale bread, crusts removed
1 cup whole walnut kernels
1-3 clove garlic, depending on size and to suit taste
½ olive oil
3 tablespoons vinegar or lemon juice
Salt and white pepper

Method
Soak the bread in a little water and press to remove excess water. It should be moist, not wet.

Place the bread, potatoes and walnuts into an electric blender and pulse until the mixture becomes a paste.

Add the garlic, salt, and gradually add the olive oil and lemon juice or vinegar.

Continue to blend, scraping the sides of the blender to ensure a smooth and consistent mixture, adding a little water if necessary.

Adjust seasoning to suit taste.

TARAMASALATA
CAVIAR DIP

Ingredients
1 tablespoon fish roe
4-6 pieces of stale white bread
¼ cup water
½ cup olive oil
¼ cup freshly squeezed lemon juice
¼ teaspoon grated onion (optional or to taste)

Method
Place all ingredients into a blender and pulse the mixture until smooth and creamy.

Make necessary adjustment to the taste to prepare the dip to your liking adding a little more olive oil, lemon juice, or water.

Transfer to a serving bowl and decorate with a sprig of fresh herbs and a pitted black olive.

Serve with lightly toasted pita bread, or crusty fresh continental bread.

TZATZIKI
YOGHURT DIP

Ingredients
1 500gm tub natural Greek yoghurt, unsweetened
1 large cucumber
1 small garlic clove, or to taste
2 tablespoons olive oil
1 tablespoon white vinegar
1 teaspoon finely chopped fresh dill or mint
¼ teaspoon white pepper
Salt to taste

Method
Place the yoghurt into a muslin cloth, or clean tea towel, tie with a piece of string and hang over a tap with a bowl beneath to capture excess liquid.

Wash the cucumber, and trim the ends, then peel and grate. Place into a strainer to drain off excess liquid.

In a bowl, place the drained yoghurt, drained cucumber, finely grated garlic, olive oil, vinegar, herbs, salt and pepper.

Make the necessary adjustments to taste, drizzle over a little olive oil, and chill ready for serving.

TYROKAFTERI
SPICY FETA DIP

Ingredients
250 grams feta, crumbled
¼ cup natural Greek yoghurt
1 teaspoons hot red peppers, chopped finely
¼ teaspoon cayenne pepper, or to taste
1 teaspoon lemon juice
2 tablespoons extra virgin olive oil
½ teaspoon parsley, finely chopped

Method
Place all ingredients into a small food processor and blend until thick and creamy. Add a little more olive oil if required.

Spoon into a bowl ready for serving, and drizzle with little olive oil, freshly cracked pepper, and a touch of finely chopped parsley.

PITA
PITA BREAD

Ingredients
1 packet of your favourite pita bread
Olive oil
Pinch of ground oregano
Freshly milled sea salt

Method
Using a pastry brush lightly paint the pita bread with a little olive oil.

Place the pita bread onto a hotplate or onto a baking tray into the oven until just slightly toasted.

Place a pinch of oregano between your hands and rub the aromatic herb over the bread, and season with a little salt.

Cut into triangles and serve immediately.

Philoxenia is more than befriending a stranger.

It encompasses the delicate art of expressing friendship, inclusion and hospitality.

MEZZE

DOLMADES
STUFFED VINE LEAVES

Ingredients
¼ cup olive oil
1 large onion, finely chopped
¾ cup long grain rice
1 cup hot water, from kettle
¼ cup tomato puree
¼ cup finely chopped parsley
¼ cup finely chopped mint
Salt and pepper, season to taste
30-50 vine leaves, depending on size

Method
Heat oil in a medium sized saucepan and sauté the onion until soft and transparent. Add the rice, stir, and cook for a couple of minutes.

Add the tomato puree, herbs, and season with salt and pepper.

Continue stirring for a minute, add hot water, bring to the boil, reduce heat and cook for approximately 5 minutes. Turn off the heat and place the lid on the pot.

To prepare the vine leaves you will need a large bowl half filled with boiling water, and another bowl filled with cold water.

Place around 5 leaves at a time into the hot water first, and using a spoon press down gently to ensure they are covered. The leaves will gradually change colour. This will take around 3-5 minutes.

Using a pair of tongs, gently remove the leaves and place into the cold water to stop the cooking process.

Take each leaf and drain over the edge of a colander that has a pan beneath it to catch the drips of water. Repeat until all leaves have been prepared. Take a vine leaf and place with the smooth side down. Add a heaped teaspoon of the mixture onto the leaf, fold in the end with the stem, fold in the opposite end, and then roll gently to form a nice little parcel.

Line the bottom of a saucepan with three layers of baking paper and a layer of vine leaves. Place the dolmades on top fitting them in nice and tight. Continue rolling until all leaves are used up.

Drizzle with approximately a quarter cup of olive oil, gently pour over three quarters of a cup hot water, and then finish with a quarter cup lemon juice.

Top the dolmades with an inverted plate to keep them from moving during the cooking process.

Place lid on pot and take to the stovetop, bring to the boil, reduce heat to low, cook for approximately one hour or until rice is tender. You'll need to have a little sneak peak to check that the dolmades are cooked through.

When ready, turn off the heat and leave the pot to sit until completely cool and all the liquid has been absorbed.

KALAMARI TIGANITO
FRIED CALAMARI

Ingredients
1 kg calamari, cleaned
Sunflower oil for frying
Lemon wedges for serving

Flour Mixture
1 teaspoon sea salt
¼ teaspoon ground black pepper
½ teaspoon dried oregano
½ cup plain flour, sifted
½ cup cornflour, sifted

Method
Carefully clean the calamari, cut into halves lengthways, the cut into 5mm strips.

In a shallow bowl combine the flour mixture ingredients.

Heat the oil in a pan until hot.

Dip the calamari into the flour mixture, shake off the excess and place into the frying pan a few at a time. Turn down the heat and cook for 1-2 minutes.

Drain well on absorbent kitchen paper and place on a serving dish with wedges of fresh lemon.

MELIZANA STI SKARA
GRILLED EGGPLANT

Ingredients
2 medium eggplants
Salt
Olive oil

Method
Rinse the eggplant, and then cut lengthways approximately 5mm thick.

Place into a colander and sprinkle with salt.

Let stand for one hour, rinse eggplant slices, and pat dry with a paper towel.

Brush the slices of eggplant with olive oil and place into a large non-stick frying pan and cook until golden brown, turning once.

Alternatively, the eggplant can be placed onto a baking tray and into a pre-heated oven. Bake until golden brown.

When cooked, season with salt and pepper, and arrange onto a serving platter. A rich homemade tomato salsa makes a good accompaniment.

GARIDES SAGANAKI
PRAWNS IN RICH TOMATO SAUCE

Ingredients
500 grams of green prawns, peeled and deveined
2 spring onions, chopped
1 clove garlic, crushed
½ cup olive oil
2 cups tomatoes, peeled and chopped
½ cup dry white wine
1 tablespoon parsley, finely chopped
½ teaspoon ground oregano
½ teaspoon sugar
Salt and pepper, to taste
Pinch of cayenne pepper (optional)
Sprinkle of feta cheese (non-fasting version)

Method
Heat the oil in a heavy based saucepan and gently sauté the spring onions for a few minutes until soft, before adding the garlic. Cook gently for 1 minute. Add all the other ingredients. Bring to the boil, lower heat and simmer until the sauce is reduced.

Transfer the sauce into a baking dish, add the prawns, mix through, and bake in a hot oven for 15-20 minutes until the prawns are cooked. Serve with fresh crusty bread, boiled rice or pasta.

KOLOKITHAKIA TIGANITIA
FRIED ZUCHINNI

Ingredients
2 medium zucchini
½ cup plain flour, seasoned with salt and pepper
1 tablespoon corn flour
Olive oil, for shallow frying
Salt
White vinegar
1 tablespoon parsley, finely chopped
1 garlic clove, peeled and coarsely chopped

Method
Rinse the zucchini and trim ends. Cut into 5mm slices either lengthways or in rounds.

In a shallow bowl place the plain flour, corn flour, salt, and pepper and mix thoroughly. Dip the zucchini into the flour mixture making sure that they are completely coated. Place onto a sheet of baking paper.

Pour enough olive oil in a frying pan to shallow fry. Heat the oil over medium heat.

When the oil is hot, working in batches, fry the zucchini until they are golden brown. Turn once during cooking process. Using a slotted spoon, transfer the fried zucchini onto absorbent paper and drain.

Arrange zucchini on a serving platter, season with salt, sprinkle with vinegar, chopped garlic and top with finely chopped parsley.

SPANAKOPITA
SPINACH PIE

Ingredients
1 packet filo pastry, or homemade filo
½ cup butter, melted (or olive oil) for brushing filo pastry
¼ cup olive oil
1 cup finely chopped spring onions
1 bunch of spinach leaves, washed and finely cut
½ cup finely chopped dill
¼ cup finely chopped mint
¼ cup finely chopped parsley
½ cup rice, par-boiled, drained and set aside
Salt and pepper

Method
Preheat the oven to 200 degrees. Grease a round *pita* tray, or other shallow baking tray with the olive oil. Heat oil in a large frying pan, sauté spring onions until soft, add spinach, herbs, salt and pepper, stir and cook until wilted. Remove from heat, and add the par-boiled rice.

Place the filo onto a clean surface brushing each sheet with butter before placing onto baking tray. Ensure that some of the filo hangs over the edges of the tray. Repeat until half the filo forms the base of the pie. Smooth the spinach mixture over the base and continue to layer with remaining filo sheets. Brush top sheet and overhanging edges of pastry with melted butter and then fold them in to form a crust around the tray. With a sharp knife proceed to lightly score the top layers of pastry into squares and using your fingers gently 'splash' some water on top of the spanakopita. Bake for 30-45 minutes, or until golden brown.

KEFTEDES
MEATBALLS

Ingredients
1 onion, finely chopped or grated
400 grams beef, minced
200 grams lamb, minced
1 egg, lightly beaten
1 tablespoon extra virgin olive oil
½ cup fresh white breadcrumbs
¼ cup parsley, finely chopped
¼ cup mint, finely chopped
1 teaspoon dried oregano
Salt and pepper
Plain flour for coating
Sunflower oil, for frying

Method
Mix together the onion, beef, lamb, egg, olive oil, breadcrumbs, herbs and seasoning. Continue mixing for 5 minutes. Cover the bowl with plastic wrap and place in the fridge for 1-2 hours. This will allow the mixture to rest and the flavours to develop.

Take a walnut size of the mixture and form a ball. Throw the ball from one hand to the other to remove air pockets. Dip the ball into the flour. Shake off any excess flour and place on a platter ready for frying. Repeat with the remainder of the mixture.

Heat the sunflower oil in a large pan, and gently fry 10-15 meatballs at a time until golden brown and cooked through, ensuring to turn once during the frying process.

A pot of soup
simmering on
the stove fills
the senses with
delight, and the
contents is
food for the soul.

SOUP

AVGOLEMONO
CHICKEN EGG LEMON SOUP

Ingredients
2 chicken carcasses, trimmed of fat, rinsed
Cooking salt
½ teaspoon whole black peppercorns
1 small whole onion (optional)
½ carrot, peeled (optional)
¼ celery stick (optional)
White rice (see note below)
1 large lemon, freshly squeezed
1 free-range egg, room temperature, separated
1 tablespoon warm water
Salt and pepper to taste

* The quantity of rice is dependent on whether you prefer your soup to have a thin or thick consistency.

Method
Bring a large pot of water to the boil and add cooking salt, chicken, and any or all of the optional vegetables.

Cover pot with lid, reduce heat, and simmer gently for 2 -3 hours until a rich stock is achieved.

Using a slotted spoon, carefully remove the chicken from the stock.

Take another pot and strain the stock through a sieve.

Bring to the boil, and add the rice. Season with a little more salt if needed. Stir well until the stock returns to a slow boil and cook until rice is tender. Be careful to not overcook the rice. Turn off heat.

Place the egg white and tablespoon of water into a glass bowl. Using an electric beater, work the egg white until stiff and firm, until it resembles a meringue. Add the egg yolk to the mixture and beat until creamy. Gradually add a quarter of the lemon juice and keep beating the mixture for 1 minute.

Whilst the beater is running, gently ladle the clear stock into the egg mixture, avoiding adding rice from the soup. Be very careful to incorporate the stock with all of the egg mixture, to prevent curdling.

Return the egg mixture carefully into the pot whilst stirring gently to incorporate. The result is a thick and creamy rice soup.

---

* For those who like to include meat in their soup replace carcasses with chicken pieces or a whole small chicken, the skin removed.

FASSOLADA
WHITE BEAN SOUP

Ingredients
2 cups dried cannellini, haricot or lima beans
7-9 cups of hot water, from the kettle
1 onion, finely chopped
1 small clove of garlic, finely chopped
2 carrots, chopped
2 celery sticks with leaves, chopped
¾ cup olive oil
1 can of whole tomatoes, pureed
1-2 tablespoons of tomato paste
¼ teaspoon ground black pepper
½ teaspoon sugar
1 teaspoon salt
Dash of cayenne pepper (optional)
2 tablespoons parsley, finely chopped

Method
Place beans on a table, check and remove any grit, transfer into a sieve, rinse and drain. Soak in a pot of cold water overnight, then drain.

In a large pot, heat the oil and fry the onion for 5 minutes, before adding carrots and celery. Continue frying for 2 minutes, stir in the garlic and fry for 1 minute. Add all other ingredients and bring to the boil. Simmer for 2 hours, or until tender. Season to taste.

FAKES
LENTIL SOUP

Ingredients
2 cups small brown lentils
1 onion, finely chopped
1 clove garlic, roughly chopped
½ cup olive oil
¼ teaspoon ground oregano
2 dried bay leaves
8 cups water
Salt and pepper
White vinegar, to serve

Method
Place lentils on a table, check and remove any grit. Transfer lentils to a sieve, rinse under cold water and drain.

Heat the olive oil in a heavy-based saucepan and gently sauté the onion until soft. Add lentils and cook for 2 minutes, stirring occasionally.

Add all other ingredients and bring to the boil.

Reduce heat and simmer for 1-2 hours, or until soup is cooked and thickened slightly.

If desired a little white vinegar can be added to the lentil soup after serving.

MANESTRA
RISONI SOUP

Ingredients
2 lamb necks or lamb shanks, trimmed of fat
1 onion whole, peeled
1 400 gram pureed tomatoes
2 tablespoons tomato paste
1 cup small pasta (risoni or vermicelli)
Salt and pepper

Method
Bring a large pot of water to the boil. Add salt, whole onion and lamb necks. Boil and skim stock using a metal spoon, reduce heat to a simmer and cook until lamb is soft and tender, approximately 2 hours. Using a sieve drain stock into a clean pot.

Return to stovetop and add pureed tomatoes, tomato paste, salt and pepper. Bring to boil. While stirring the stock gradually add the pasta.

Bring to the boil, reduce heat, and continue cooking until the pasta is al dente.

* For a healthier version, leave stock overnight for fat to solidify. Next day remove fat that has come to surface. Reheat before adding pasta.

* For a vegan version omit the lamb, replace with a good quality vegan stock powder.

TOMATO SOUPA
TOMATO SOUP WITH PASTA

Ingredients
4 medium tomatoes
6 cups water
1 carrot, peeled and sliced
1 stalk celery, peeled
1 parsley sprig
¼ olive oil
Salt and pepper
1 cup pasta (risoni or vermicelli)

Method
Place tomatoes into a bowl of hot water, and leave for a few minutes before removing. Using the blunt side of a sharp knife proceed to press firmly around the tomato to loosen the skin from the fruit. Using the sharp side of the knife make an incision into the tomato and proceed to remove the skin. Set tomatoes aside. Cut the tomatoes into quarters, scoop out seeds, and discard.

Place tomatoes, water, carrot, celery, parsley, olive oil and salt and pepper into a heavy based saucepan. Bring to the boil, reduce to a simmer and cover saucepan with lid slightly ajar. Continue to simmer on low for approximately 40 minutes.

Strain the stock through a sieve and return to saucepan. Bring to boil and add pasta, reduce heat and continue to cook until the pasta is ready. Check seasoning and adjust accordingly.

SOUPA ME MANITARIA
MUSHROOM SOUP / VEGAN MAGERITSA

Ingredients
500 grams mushrooms, both white and brown, chopped
2 spring onions, finely chopped
1 leek, finely chopped
1 small Cos lettuce, chopped
¼ cup olive oil
¼ cup dry white wine
½ cup fresh dill, chopped
1 tablespoon fresh mint, chopped
6 cups hot water from kettle
1 teaspoon vegan chicken stock powder
Salt and pepper
½ teaspoon, dried chili flakes (optional)
¼ cup rice (optional)
Juice of 1 lemon
2 teaspoons corn flour

Method
Heat olive oil in saucepan, sauté spring onions and leek until soft, add mushrooms and sauté for 3 minutes. Deglaze pan with the wine before adding hot water, stock, lettuce, dill, mint, salt and pepper. Bring stock to boil. Reduce heat, replace lid and simmer until cooked. Add rice and continue to simmer for 15-20 minutes until cooked.

Place the cornflour into a cup together with a little water to make a thin paste and add 2-3 tablespoons of lemon juice. Carefully add the mixture to the soup all the while continuing to mix through to avoid any lumps. Season to taste. Sprinkle with a little freshly chopped dill.

Since ancient times banquets were organised to welcome visitors.

Not much has changed since then.

MAINS

ARNI YAHNI
BRAISED LAMB

Ingredients
¼ cup olive oil
1 onion, finely chopped
1 kg boned shoulder of lamb
½ red wine
440 gram tin pureed tomatoes
2 tablespoons tomato paste
1-2 bay leaves
2 inch cinnamon stick
3 cloves or 3 pimento
1 teaspoon sugar
¼ teaspoon ground cayenne pepper (optional)
1½ cups of hot water, from kettle
Salt and pepper to taste

Method
In a heavy based saucepan, heat oil and sauté onion for 2-3 minutes before adding the lamb and browning on all sides. Pour in the wine and stir well.

Add all other ingredients, bring to the boil, cover pot, reduce heat, and cook gently for 2 to 2 ½ hour or until lamb is tender.

Serve braised lamb with boiled spaghetti, tubular pasta, or boiled rice.

KOTOPOULO KOKKINISTO
BRAISED CHICKEN

Ingredients
¼ cup olive oil
1 onion, finely chopped
2 kg chicken pieces, skin removed
½ white wine
440 gram tin whole tomatoes, roughly chopped
2 tablespoons tomato paste
1 bay leaf
2 inch cinnamon stick
3 cloves or 3 pimento
1 teaspoon sugar
¼ teaspoon ground cayenne pepper (optional)
1½ cups of hot water, from kettle
Salt and pepper to taste

Method
In a heavy based saucepan, heat oil and sauté onion for 2-3 minutes before adding the chicken and browning on all sides. Pour in the wine and stir well. Add all other ingredients, bring to the boil, cover pot, reduce heat, and cook gently for 1 to 1 ½ hour or until chicken is tender.

Serve braised chicken with boiled spaghetti, tubular pasta, or boiled rice.

PSITO ARNI
ROAST LAMB

Ingredients
1 leg or shoulder of lamb
2 cloves garlic, cut into slits
½ cup olive oil
4 tablespoons dried oregano
¼ cup salt
2 teaspoons black ground pepper
2 cups hot water
4-6 potatoes cut into 6 wedges
Juice of 2 lemons

Method
Preheat oven to 200 degrees.

Trim any excess fat from lamb, cut slits, and insert slices of garlic. Place the lamb into a baking dish, pour over the olive oil and sprinkle with oregano. Season with salt and pepper, and massage the seasoning onto the lamb. Pour hot water into the baking dish, and place into hot oven for 30 minutes. Turn the lamb over, and if required add a little more hot water to cover the base of the dish. Cover baking dish tightly with foil, to keep the juices sealed. Return to oven and reduce heat to a moderate temperature, and bake for 1½ to 2 hours, depending on size of lamb.

Add potatoes, and season with salt, pepper and oregano. Pour the lemon juice over the lamb and potatoes.

Cover again and cook until the lamb is tender and potatoes are cooked.

PSARI TIGANITO
FRIED FISH

Ingredients
500 grams Fish fillets (garfish, whiting, flathead or similar)
½ cup sunflower oil, for frying
Lemon wedges for serving

Flour Mixture
1 teaspoon sea salt
¼ teaspoon ground black pepper
½ teaspoon dried oregano
½ cup plain flour, sifted
½ cup cornflour, sifted

Method
Heat the oil in a pan until hot.

In a shallow bowl combine the flour mixture ingredients.

Dip the fish into the flour mixture, shake off the excess and place into the frying pan a few at a time. Turn down the heat and cook for a few minutes on either side.

Transfer to a plate lined with absorbent paper, before placing onto a serving dish with wedges of fresh lemon.

*If using whole fish, ensure it is cleaned and descaled. Using a sharp knife score both sides of fish, and sprinkle salt into the cavity. Dip into flour mixture before shallow frying.

BAKALIAROS YAHNI
COD STEW

Ingredients
¼ cup olive oil
1 onion, finely chopped
500 grams dried salted cod
4 medium potatoes cut into quarters
440 gram tin pureed tomatoes
2 tablespoons tomato paste
¼ teaspoon ground cayenne pepper (optional)
1½ cups of hot water, from kettle
Salt and pepper to taste

Method
Remove the skin from the cod and cut into 5-inch pieces. Rinse off the salt and place into a glass bowl. Soak the cod in water for approximately 12 hours in the refrigerator, making sure to change the water several times.

Drain and remove any visible bones, and then allow the cod to drain.

In a heavy based saucepan, heat oil and sauté onion for 5 minutes or until soft. Add the tomatoes, tomato paste, seasoning and water and bring to the boil. Cover pot, reduce heat, and cook gently for 20 minutes.

Add potatoes and cod, bring pot to the boil, reduce heat and simmer for 30-45 minutes or until cooked.

For the Greeks, food is not only about using the freshest and in-season produce. It's love on a plate.

It's about sharing and caring. It's about nourishing the spirit and the soul.

It is a lifestyle of unique rituals and ancient traditions shared with family and friends.

It's about cooking slow, eating for enjoyment, and living with passion.

KALAMARI KOKKINISTO
BRAISED CALAMARI

Ingredients
500 grams calamari, cleaned, cut into strips
1 large onion, diced
¼ cup olive oil
1 400 gram tin of chopped tomatoes
1 cup hot water from kettle
3 bay leaves
2 cinnamon quills
5 clove buds
½ teaspoon whole black peppercorns
¼ teaspoon cayenne pepper
Salt

Method
Heat a frying pan that has not been oiled, add the calamari and cook for a few minutes until it changes colour and juices have evaporated. Turn off heat and set aside.

In a heavy based saucepan heat the oil and gently, fry onion until transparent, and add the spices stirring gently to reveal their aromas. Pour in the chopped tomatoes, hot water and calamari. Bring to the boil, reduce heat and simmer for 1½ hours, or until tender and the sauce is thick and rich.

Serve with boiled rice, pilafi, pasta, or fresh bread.

PSARI PLAKI
BAKED FISH

Ingredients
1 whole white flesh fish such as snapper
2 tablespoons fresh lemon juice
½ cup olive oil
1 medium onion, sliced
1 cup pureed tomatoes
1 medium tomato, sliced
½ cup dry white wine
¼ cup parsley, finely chopped
Salt and pepper

Method
Preheat the oven to 180 degrees. Heat the oil in a heavy based saucepan and sauté onion until soft, and add the pureed tomatoes, wine, half the parsley, salt and pepper. Simmer for 30 minutes.

Ensure the fish has been cleaned and descaled. Make an incision on each side of the fish. Place the fish into a large baking dish that has been greased with a little olive oil. Drizzle lemon juice over the fish and season the fish and the cavity with salt and pepper.

Pour over the tomato and onion mixture making sure to cover the entire fish. Top with slices of tomatoes, sprinkle with parsley, and drizzle with olive oil.

Cover with foil and bake in oven for half an hour. Remove the foil and continue to bake for another 30 minutes, until the fish is tender and sauce has thickened.

FASSOLAKIA ME PATATES
GREEN BEAN AND POTATO STEW

Ingredients
500 grams stringless green beans, trimmed
1/2 cup olive oil
1 large onion, finely chopped
1 clove garlic, crushed
1 tin whole tomatoes, pureed
1 cup water, hot
3 large potatoes cut into 6 wedges
2 medium carrots cut into 2cm rounds (optional)
Salt and pepper
Pinch cayenne pepper (optional)
2 tablespoons chopped parsley

Method
Heat the olive oil in a large pot and sauté the onion until soft.

Add the beans, sauté for a few minutes, then add garlic, and stir for 1 minute.

Add tomatoes, potatoes, water, salt, pepper and parsley, and cook until the vegetables are tender.

Season to taste.

PASTITSIO
MACARONI AND MEAT PIE

Ingredients
500 grams long tubular pasta, cooked in boiling salted water until tender, and drained.
2 free-range organic eggs, separated (keep yolks for white sauce)
¾ cup grated cheese (kefalotiri, or pecorino)

Meat Sauce
1 onion, finely chopped
2 tablespoons butter
2 tablespoons olive oil
250 grams ground beef
250 grams ground lamb
1 clove garlic, crushed
1 cinnamon stick
½ cup wine (red or white, room temperature)
400 gram tin of whole tomatoes, pureed
1 cup tomato puree
3 tablespoons tomato paste
1 cup hot water or stock
3 tablespoons parsley, finely chopped
½ teaspoon sugar
Pinch of cayenne pepper (optional
Salt and pepper

White Sauce
¾ cup of butter
½ cup plain flour
3 cups milk, hot
¼ teaspoon grated nutmeg
Salt and pepper
2 egg yolks

Method

Meat Sauce
In a heavy based saucepan heat the olive oil and butter, and gently fry onion until soft. Increase heat and add the ground beef and lamb, stirring well until meat begins to brown. Add garlic and cook for 1 minute. Add wine, stir well, and then all other ingredients, bring to the boil, cover, reduce heat and simmer gently for 1½ to 2 hours until the sauce is rich and thick. Season to taste, and set aside to cool.

White Sauce
In a heavy based saucepan melt the butter, and stir in the flour and cook for 2 minutes. Gradually add hot milk whilst stirring and continue mixing over the heat until the white sauce is thick, smooth and lump free before adding ground nutmeg, and season with salt and pepper to taste. Remove from heat, and cool, before quickly mixing in the 2 egg yolks. Set aside to cool.

To assemble
Butter an oven dish 13 x 9 x 3 or similar. Beat the egg whites until thick and stiff, and set aside.

Mix the meat sauce through the cooked pasta. Mix the beaten egg whites through pasta and meat sauce. Spread the mixture evenly into the baking dish. Gently spoon over the white sauce and spread to evenly cover the pasta.

Sprinkle with grated cheese and cook in a moderate oven for 45 minutes to one hour or until golden brown. Let stand for 15 minutes before serving.

* This dish has successfully been modified to a vegan version. Simply replace meat with 2 tins of drained and rinsed lentils, and substitute butter for non-dairy butter, and dairy milk with oat milk. Omit egg, and if desired use a vegan cheese.

MOUSSAKA
AUBERGINE WITH MEAT SAUCE

Ingredients
2 -3 large eggplants

Meat Sauce
1 onion, finely chopped
2 tablespoons butter
2 tablespoons olive oil
250 grams ground beef
250 grams ground lamb
1 clove garlic, crushed
1 cinnamon stick
½ cup wine (red or white, room temperature)
1 400 gram tin of whole tomatoes, pureed
1 cup tomato puree
2 tablespoons tomato paste
1 cup hot water or stock
3 tablespoons parsley, finely chopped
½ teaspoon sugar
Pinch of cayenne pepper (optional)
Salt and pepper

White Sauce
¾ cup of butter
½ cup plain flour
3 cups milk, hot
¼ teaspoon ground cinnamon
3 tablespoons grated cheese (kefalotiri or pecorino)
Salt and pepper
1 egg, lightly beaten

Method
Cut eggplant lengthways into thin slices approximately 5mm. Sprinkle with salt and place in colander for approximately 1 hour. Rinse, and then pat dry with paper towels. Brush the eggplant slices with a little olive oil and either grill in an oven or shallow fry until brown.

Meat Sauce
In a heavy based saucepan heat the olive oil and butter, and gently fry onion until soft. Increase heat and add the ground beef and lamb, stirring well until meat begins to brown. Add garlic and cook for 1 minute. Add wine, stir well, and then add all other ingredients, bring to the boil, cover, reduce heat and simmer gently for 1½ to 2 hours until the sauce is rich and thick. Season to taste, and set aside to cool.

White Sauce
In a heavy based saucepan melt the butter, and stir in the flour and cook for 2 minutes. Gradually add hot milk whilst stirring and continue mixing over the heat until the white sauce is thick, smooth and lump free before adding ground cinnamon, 1 tablespoon of grated cheese, and season with salt and pepper to taste. Remove from heat, and cool, before quickly mixing in the egg.

To Assemble
Grease an oven dish approximately 13x9x2 and line with a layer of eggplant. Pour half the meat sauce and spread evenly. Add another layer of eggplant, followed by another layer of meat sauce, and finish with a layer of eggplant. Spread the white sauce evenly over the top and sprinkle with remaining cheese. Bake in a moderate over for approximately 45 minutes to 1 hour or until golden in colour.

Let stand for 15 minutes before serving.

* This dish has successfully been modified to a vegan version. Simply replace meat with 2 tins of drained and rinsed lentils, and substitute butter for non-dairy butter, and dairy milk with oat milk. Omit egg, and if desired use a vegan cheese.

BRIAMI
BAKED VEGETABLES

Ingredients
1 large onion, peeled and sliced
2 medium zucchini, sliced
1 medium red capsicum, sliced
1 large eggplant, cut into eight
5 large potatoes, cut into six wedges
2 cups tomatoes, peeled and chopped
¼ cup chopped parsley
½ cup olive oil
½ teaspoon sugar
1 teaspoon sea salt
¼ teaspoon ground black pepper
Pinch of cayenne (optional)

Method
Preheat oven to 180 degrees.

Wash the eggplant and cut into eight pieces, before placing into a colander and sprinkling with salt. Leave for 1 hour, rinse, and pat dry.

In the meantime, prepare all other vegetables and herbs and place into a baking dish. Rinse the eggplant and add to dish with all remaining ingredients and mix well. Bake for 1 to 1 ½ hours in a moderate oven until all ingredients are cooked through.

YEMISTA
RICE STUFFED VEGETABLES

Ingredients
6 ripe tomatoes
3 green capsicums
3 red capsicums
3 potatoes, peeled and cut into wedges

Stuffing
¼ cup olive oil
2 medium onions, finely chopped
2 cloves of garlic, chopped
2 cups short grain rice
3 cups hot water, from kettle
2 tablespoons tomato paste
1/2 cup parsley, finely chopped
¼ cup mint, finely chopped
¼ cup basil leaves, roughly chopped
1½ teaspoons dried oregano
Salt and pepper

Topping
¼ cup olive oil
1 cup water
1 tablespoon tomato paste
Salt, pepper, dried oregano

Method
Drizzle a little olive oil into a baking pan.

Slice the tops of the tomatoes three quarters of the way across. Using a small spoon scoop out the pulp, placing it into a sieve to separate the pulp from the seeds. Use a spoon to press the pulp through the sieve and reserve the juice. Discard the tomato seeds.

Place the capsicums on their sides and slice three quarters of the way across. Using a small knife carefully scrape out seeds and pith. Arrange the vegetables onto the baking tray sprinkling a little salt into the cavities. Set aside.

Preheat oven to 200 degrees.

In a heavy based large frying pan heat the oil and sauté onions until soft and transparent. Add the rice and stir thoroughly. Add garlic and sauté for one minute before adding the reserved tomato pulp, tomato paste, water, and herbs. Season with salt and pepper, and simmer until the rice is partially cooked. Make sure that a little liquid remains in the pan.

Spoon the rice mixture into the vegetables being careful to not fill them up too much before replacing the tops on the vegetables.

Place the potato wedges into a bowl. Drizzle with olive oil, and sprinkle with salt, dried oregano and ground black pepper. Mix thoroughly before placing the wedges in between the stuffed vegetables.

In a jug combine the water, tomato paste, and olive oil, and season with salt and pepper. Carefully spoon the tomato mixture over the vegetables making sure to coat each one. Sprinkle the vegetables evenly with dried oregano.

Cover with foil and bake for 40 minutes. Remove foil, baste vegetables with pan juices and return to oven. Bake for a further 30 to 40 minutes or until vegetables are tender and rice is cooked. Yemista can be served hot or cold. The flavour develops when left to stand a while.

* Zucchini can also be used to prepare these delicious stuffed vegetables, or you may prefer to only use one type of seasonal vegetables. Experiment and have fun!

MELIZANES LADERA
BAKED EGGPLANT

Ingredients
6 eggplants, preferably long variety
¾ cup olive oil
2 medium onions, sliced thinly
3-4 garlic cloves, sliced into slivers
¼ cup parsley, chopped
1½ cups tomatoes,
1 tablespoon sugar

Method
Preheat oven to 180 degrees.

Wash eggplants, cut off the green end, and make a slit lengthways in each one. Soak in a bowl of salted water for one hour. Drain and dry well with absorbent paper.

Heat the oil in a large frying pan and fry eggplants gently over low heat, Turn once and continue frying until they begin to soften. Remove from pan and set aside.

Add the onions to the pan and fry gently until onion is soft and transparent. Add the garlic and cook for one minute, before adding all other ingredients. Mix ingredients through, and simmer for 20 minutes.

Place the cooked eggplants close together into a greased oven dish and fill the incisions with the tomato mixture. Pour remaining mixture over the eggplant. Cover the dish with foil and bake in a moderate oven for 45 minutes or until cooked through.

KOUNOUPIDI YAHNI
BRAISED CAULIFLOWER

Ingredients
¼ cup olive oil
1/2 cauliflower head, cut into florets
1 onion, finely
1 cinnamon quill
2 pimento or clove buds
1 400gm tin pureed tomatoes
¼ cup cooking sherry or red wine
¼ cup water
Salt and pepper, to taste
Pinch of cayenne pepper (optional)

Method
Bring a pot of water to the boil, add a teaspoon of salt and cook the cauliflower for 5 minutes. Drain and rinse to stop cooking process.

In a saucepan, heat the olive oil, and sauté the onions until soft.

Add the tomatoes, cinnamon stick, salt and pepper. Bring to the boil, and add the sherry. Cook for 2 minutes.

Add the water and cook on moderate heat for 15 minutes before adding the cauliflower. Reduce the heat to a low simmer and cook until cauliflower is tender.

PATATES YAHNI
BRAISED POTATOES

Ingredients
4 Potatoes, peeled and cut into wedges
1 large onion, thinly sliced
¾ cup olive oil
¾ cup tomato salsa
2 cups hot water from kettle
Salt and pepper
2 tablespoons parsley, finely chopped
Cayenne pepper (optional)

Method
In a heavy based saucepan heat the oil and sauté the onion until soft and transparent.

Add the potatoes, tomato salsa, hot water, parsley, and season with salt and pepper. Mix gently and bring to boil.

Reduce heat and simmer for 30-45 or until potatoes are cooked and the sauce is rich and thick.

SPANAKORIZO
SPINACH WITH RICE

Ingredients

1 bunch spinach
1/2 cup olive oil
1 cup medium grain rice
1 cup spring onion, chopped
1/4 cup fresh dill, cut finely
1/4 cup fresh parsley, cut finely
2 cups hot water from the kettle
Lemon wedges

Method

Wash and rinse the spinach well, and roughly chop.

Heat the oil in a heavy-based saucepan and sauté the spring onions for a few minutes. Stir in the rice. Cook for 2-3 minutes. Add the chopped spinach and stir to mix through before adding the hot water and herbs.

Season with salt and pepper and continue to cook over low heat. When ready, remove from the heat and serve immediately with a wedge of lemon.

Alternatively, for a tomato-based recipe add some tomato salsa or paste with the hot water, and omit the lemon.

RIZI ME KANELLA
CINNAMON RICE

Ingredients
4 tablespoons olive oil
2 tablespoons butter (or non-dairy vegan spread)
1 onion, finely chopped
½ cup celery stalks, finely chopped
¾ cup short grain rice
1 cup vegetable stock, hot
½ cup currants
½ cup chopped blanched almonds
2 cups chopped walnuts
½ teaspoon ground cinnamon
1 tablespoon finely chopped parsley
Salt and pepper

Method
In a heavy based saucepan heat the butter and olive oil, and gently fry onion for 5 minutes or until soft. Add the celery and continue frying gently for 5 minutes. Stir in the rice and fry for 1-2 minutes.

Add the vegetable stock, stir and bring to the boil, cover pan, reduce heat, and cook until ready. Check if more liquid is required to cook rice.

Remove from heat, and mix in all remaining ingredients. Season to taste.

MACARONIA ME TOMATA SALSA
MACARONI WITH TOMATO SALSA

Ingredients
500gm pasta thin spaghetti
3 tablespoons extra virgin oil
1 400gm tin pureed tomatoes
1 cinnamon stick
3 clove buds
¼ red wine
Salt and pepper
Dash of cayenne pepper (optional)

Method
Bring a large pot of water to the boil, and add salt.

Add the pasta, stirring occasionally and cook following the packet directions, until slightly firm (al dente).

Transfer to colander, and drain.

Heat the oil in a heavy based pan.

Add the pureed tomatoes, wine, cinnamon stock and cloves.

Bring to the boil before adding the red wine. Stir gently.

Season to taste, reduce heat and simmer for 20-30 minutes or until rich and thick.

MACARONIA ME TIRI
MACARONI WITH CHEESE

Ingredients
500gm pasta (thin or tubular spaghetti)
3 tablespoons extra virgin olive oil
¾ cup Myzythra cheese, grated finely
Salt and white pepper, to taste

Method
Bring a large pot of water to the boil, and add salt.

Add the pasta, stirring occasionally and cook following the packet directions, until slightly firm (al dente).

Transfer to colander, and drain.

Return the empty pot to a low heat over the stove to evaporate any remaining liquid.

Gently pour in a little olive oil and warm before returning the pasta. Stir through ensuring the pasta is fully coated.

Transfer to a serving dish, sprinkle with pepper and Myzythra cheese.

MACARONIA ME KIMA
MACARONI WITH MINCE SAUCE

Ingredients
500 grams minced beef
250 grams minced lamb
¼ cup olive oil
1 large onion, finely chopped
1 clove garlic, chopped
400 gram tin chopped tomatoes
½ cup red wine
½ cup tomato salsa (bottled)
1 cup hot water from kettle
¼ cup parsley, finely chopped
1 cinnamon quill
2 bay leaves
½ teaspoon sugar
Salt and pepper
Cayenne pepper (optional)
Myzithra cheese for sprinkling on top

Method
In a heavy based saucepan heat olive oil and gently fry onion until soft. Increase heat add ground beef and lamb, stirring well until meat begins to brown. Add garlic and cook for 1 minute. Add wine, stir well, and then add all other ingredients. Bring to the boil, cover, reduce heat and simmer gently for 1½ to 2 hours until the sauce is rich and thick. Season to taste.

Serve with your favourite pasta, and a bowl of Myzithra cheese to sprinkle on top.

REVITHIA YAHNI
BRAISED CHICKPEAS

Ingredients
¼ cup olive oil
1 finely chopped onion
400 gram tin pureed tomatoes
400 gram tin chickpeas, or fresh soaked overnight
¼ cup red wine or port wine
2 cups hot water, from kettle
2 tablespoons fresh parsley, chopped
1 teaspoon dried oregano
1 bay leaf
Salt, pepper, to taste
Cayenne pepper, to taste (optional)
Extra parsley

Method
Heat olive oil in a heavy based saucepan, add onion and sauté until soft. Stir in the tomatoes, red wine, herbs, seasoning, and cook for 2 minutes.

Add water and simmer for 30 minutes before adding the canned chickpeas. Stir occasionally and continue cooking until the sauce is thick and rich and the chickpeas are tender.

Stir in parsley and cook for a few more minutes.

* If using soaked chickpeas the cooking time will be longer

Legumes, freshly picked fruits and vegetables are central to the highly regarded Mediterranean Diet.

SALADS

BROCOLLO
BROCOLLI SALAD

Ingredients
Broccoli
Salt
Olive oil
Lemon juice

Method
Wash the broccoli well and then peel and slice the stems, and cut into florets.

Place 2 inches of water into a pot and bring to the boil before adding salt.

Place the broccoli into the pot, replace the lid, and lower the heat.

Cook until tender, drain and rinse under cold water to finish the cooking process.

Return the empty pot to the stove on the lowest heat, adding the broccoli for a minute or two to evaporate the remaining water.

Transfer to a serving bowl, sprinkle with a little salt, drizzle with olive oil and fresh lemon juice.

FASSOLIA SALATA
GREEN BEAN SALAD

Ingredients
250 grams green stringless beans, topped and tailed
Salt
Parsley, finely chopped
1 clove garlic, or more to suit taste
Extra virgin olive oil
White vinegar

Method
Bring a pot of water to the boil, add a heaped teaspoon of salt, and the green beans.

Cook until tender and then drain in a colander, before rinsing with cold water to finish the cooking process.

Drain well, before placing into a serving dish.

Sprinkle with chopped garlic and parsley, add a little more salt if desired.

Drizzle with olive oil and vinegar and mix through.

KOUNOUPIDI SALATA
CAULIFLOWER SALAD

Ingredients
Half a head of cauliflower
Salt
Olive oil
White wine vinegar

Method
Wash the cauliflower well and cut into florets.

Place 2 inches of water into a pot and bring to the boil before adding salt.

Place the cauliflower into the pot, replace the lid, and lower the heat.

Cook until tender, drain and rinse under cold water to finish the cooking process.

Return the empty pot to the stove on the lowest heat, adding the cauliflower for a minute or two to evaporate the remaining water.

Transfer to a serving bowl, sprinkle with a little salt, drizzle with olive oil and white wine vinegar.

PATATA SALATA
POTATO SALAD

Ingredients
4 large potatoes, peeled and cut into cubes
½ teaspoon dried oregano
½ teaspoon dried mint
¼ cup flat leaf parsley, finely chopped
½ cup extra virgin olive oil
1 tablespoon white wine vinegar
1 tablespoon red onion, chopped roughly (optional)
Salt and pepper

Method
Bring a pot of water to the boil add salt and potatoes. Bring to boil and reduce heat a little. Cook until tender.

Drain the potatoes and rinse in cold water.

Transfer the potatoes to a serving bowl and add the parsley, mint, oregano and onion.

Season with salt and pepper, and then drizzle with olive oil and white vinegar, to taste.

PANTZARIA
BEETROOT SALAD

Ingredients
1 bunch of beetroot
Extra virgin olive oil
Vinegar – red or white
1 clove roughly chopped garlic (optional)

Method
Take the whole bunch of beetroot and cut off the greens. Wash and rinse several times to ensure that no dirt remains. Separate the red stems and trim into 3cm pieces. Place into a separate bowl. Roughly chop the leaves, putting them aside in a separate bowl.

Scrub the beets well, peel and cut into quarters before cooking in boil salted water for approximately 20 minutes or until half cooked. Add the stems, and cook for a further 5 minutes, and then add the leaves and cook until the beets are tender.

Drain into colander, and rinse under cold water.

Drain well before placing into a serving bowl and dress to taste with extra virgin olive oil, vinegar, salt, and garlic if used.

HORTA
BOILED GREENS

Ingredients
1 bunch Leafy Greens (Amaranthus, Dandelions, Silverbeet, or Endive)
Extra Virgin Olive Oil
Lemon Juice or Vinegar
Salt

Method
Place a large pot half filled with water on the stove and bring to the boil.

Wash the leafy greens well, and remove any discoloured leaves. If using the stalks of the Silverbeet, cut them roughly and set aside for par boiling before adding leaves to the pot.

Add a teaspoon of salt to the pot and then carefully add the washed leafy greens. Stir and then bring to the boil before reducing the heat slightly to a slow boil. Cook for approximately 20 minutes, or until tender. Dandelion leaves take longer to cook.

When ready, empty the pot into a colander and drain well, or before draining reserve some of the cooking stock for a nutritious drink to be enjoyed with a splash of fresh lemon juice.

Place the horta into a shallow open serving bowl and dress with a generous amount of extra virgin olive oil, and either lemon juice or vinegar, and a sprinkling of salt.

HORIATIKI SALATA
GREEK SALAD

Ingredients
4 ripe tomatoes, cut into wedges or slices
2 small cucumbers, semi peeled and diced
¼ cup red onion, thinly sliced
1 long green pepper or capsicum, sliced
½ cup of Kalamata olives
1 teaspoon dried oregano
1 slice feta cheese
Extra virgin olive oil
White vinegar (optional)
Salt and pepper

Method
Place the tomatoes onto an open flat salad platter, and season with a little pepper and oregano.

Top with the slices of red onion, capsicums and diced cucumbers, and sprinkle with salt.

Scatter the olives on top.

Sprinkle a little more oregano and then drizzle with a good amount of extra virgin olive oil and a little white vinegar, if used.

Place feta cheese on top.

* I prefer to peel my tomatoes, and gently squeeze out the seeds.

MAROULI SALATA
LETTUCE SALAD

Ingredients
1 Cos lettuce, or your favourite leafy greens
1 tablespoon chopped fresh dill or mint
Extra virgin olive oil
White vinegar or lemon juice
Salt

Method
Wash each lettuce leaf well, and drain in a colander.

Chop the lettuce leaves finely and place into a serving bowl.

Top with finely cut fresh dill or mint, and season to taste.

Drizzle with olive oil and white vinegar or lemon juice.

MAPA SALATA
GREEK COLESLAW

Ingredients
¼ white cabbage, shredded
1 carrot, peeled and grated
½ small red capsicum, chopped finely
½ cup parsley, chopped finely
Extra virgin olive oil
White vinegar or lemon juice
Salt and pepper, to taste

Method
In a salad bowl place the shredded cabbage, grated carrots, sliced capsicum and parsley, and mix well.

Sprinkle with a salt and drizzle with olive oil and white vinegar or lemon juice, and toss through.

Nothing quite says summer like a juicy wedge of watermelon.

FRUIT

FRUITA
FRUITS

Fresh seasonal fruit makes a delightful finale to a meal, and this is especially true for the Greeks who espouse the Mediterranean diet. They much prefer partaking of ripe and luscious fruit for dessert rather than sweets.

Each season brings forth its own unique and colourful bounty packed with nutrients and goodness that is food not just for the body but also for the soul. Locally grown and sourced is good, but home grown is great! The flavour, fragrance and freshness of fruit that has been harvested from ones own garden cannot compare to any store bought produce.

Nothing heralds summer more than platters piled high with wedges of pink, sweet, juicy watermelon. There are times that I like to add another layer of flavour with a sprinkling of freshly harvested mint leaves and a squeeze of lemon juice.

Ground black pepper pairs beautifully with chilled rockmelon. The warmth and spiciness of the pepper brings out the sweetness of the melon, and the colour of this popular spice provides a pleasant visual contrast against this orange coloured fruit.

As the weather warms up, grape vines produce their luscious smooth-skinned fruit in various hues from black, crimson, purple and white. These delightful table grapes bursting with flavour and sweetness make a refreshing snack to be enjoyed anytime of the day.

Aromatic stone fruit, be it peaches, nectarines, plums or apricots, usually ripen quite quickly, and mostly all at the same time. What can't be eaten or shared with loved ones is preserved as conserves or jams, to be enjoyed throughout the year as a condiment for fresh bread or toast, or served with fresh natural yoghurt.

In autumn sliced up apples and pears are made even more aromatic with the addition of a sprinkling of ground cinnamon. Figs harvested in the early hours of the morning, is an experience like no other. Enjoyed at their peak in their purest form is heaven on a plate. Alternatively, these luscious fruits can be sliced and served over rusks that have been spread with a little *Myzithra* cheese, making for a lovely, yet simple summer breakfast.

The aromatic flavours of citrus fruits are what nature provides in the winter months. Fresh oranges and mandarins are packed with important vitamins for health and wellbeing.

Lemons are available year round and these aromatic fruits are one of the most important ingredients in Greek cuisine, squeezed freshly over salads, vegetables, meat, poultry and fish, and used in syrups to be poured over cakes infusing the sweets with a delightful citrusy flavour and perfume. Slices of the sunny coloured fruit together with a squeeze of juice can be added to a jug of water making a refreshing drink with added health benefits!

For the Greeks, food, drink and hospitality are an expression of welcoming people into one's home.

COFFEE

GREEK COFFEE

To prepare Greek coffee you will need an appropriate sized *briki* and a long handled teaspoon, and demitasse coffee cups to serve.

Using a demitasse coffee cup, add the required number of cups of water into the *briki,* filled to just shy of the top of the cup, followed by the desired amount of sugar and one heaped teaspoon of coffee per person.

Take the *briki* to the stovetop and using a long handled teaspoon, begin to stir the pot until the sugar is dissolved.

Allow the coffee to rise to the top of the *briki.* A wonderful creamy froth will appear. This is called *kaimaki* (pronounced kay-maki) and you must act quickly so as to not lose this creamy froth. It's what distinguishes a well-made Greek coffee.

Immediately take the *briki* off the heat and proceed to pour a small amount of froth into the cups. This allows the even distribution of the *kaimaiki*.

Continue to top up the cups with the remainder of the coffee.

Serve immediately with a glass of cold water.

FRAPPE KAFE
Iced Coffee Frappe

Ingredients
1 teaspoon good quality instant coffee
Sugar to taste
1 tablespoon water
Cold milk or Cold water, as preferred

Method
Place the coffee, sugar, and one tablespoon of water into a tall glass. Blend together using a hand held milk frother until the mixture becomes thick and creamy.

Place several ice-cubes into the glass, and pour in the iced water or milk.

Frappe Kafe is a delicious and refreshing cold coffee beverage, especially enjoyed in the warmer months.

*Recipe per person

There are times that all we really need is to indulge in the tiniest morsel of something sweet.

SWEETS

BOUGHATSA
BAKED PASTRY WITH CUSTARD

Ingredients

Custard
¼ cup butter
2/3 cup fine semolina
4 cups milk, hot
2/3 cup sugar
2 egg yolks
1 teaspoon pure vanilla essence

Filo
500gm filo pastry
2/3 cup unsalted butter
Ground cinnamon
Icing sugar

Method
Preheat oven to 180 degrees.

In a heavy based saucepan, melt the butter, add the semolina, milk and sugar and stir well, until the mixture thickens. Remove from heat. Working quickly, add the egg yolks and vanilla essence and stir well.

Place a piece of cling wrap or buttered baking paper over the custard mixture to prevent skin forming, and cool.

Melt the butter and then lay out the filo pastry onto a clean board or bench. Using a brush dipped into the melted butter grease a baking tray 13 x 9 x 2 inches.

Line the base of the baking tray with half of the quantity of filo pastry, brushing each sheet with melted butter.

Before placing the last sheet on the base layer, sprinkle the previous filo layer with a good sprinkling of ground cinnamon and icing sugar. Add the last sheet, and then pour the cooled custard mixture on top.

Add a layer of filo pastry, and once again sprinkle ground cinnamon and icing sugar on top, before proceeding to finish off layering the buttered filo sheets on top, ensuring that the top layer is buttered.

Using a sharp knife, score the top 3 layers of pastry in your preferred shape of either squares or diamonds.

To finish, using a sharp knife trim the edges, or butter the untrimmed filo edges and fold them in to form a crust around the edge of the dish. Bake in a moderate over for 45 minutes or until golden brown. Remove from oven and cool.

To serve, sprinkle liberally with icing sugar.

KOLOKITHOPITA

PUMPKIN PIE

Ingredients
1 packet of filo pastry, or handmade pastry
½ cup butter, melted
2 cups grated pumpkin
½ cup fine semolina
¾ cup sugar
2 teaspoons ground cinnamon
1/3 cup currants or sultanas

Syrup (optional)
2 tablespoons honey
½ sugar
½ cup water

Method
Preheat oven to 180 degrees.

In a bowl mix the grated pumpkin, semolina, sugar, cinnamon and currants or sultanas.

Melt the butter and then lay out the filo pastry onto a clean board or bench. Using a pastry brush dipped in the melted butter grease a shallow baking tray.

Line the base of the baking tray with half of the quantity of filo pastry, brushing each sheet with melted butter.

Evenly spread the pumpkin mixture and proceed to finish off layering the buttered filo sheets on top, ensuring that the top layer is buttered.

Using a sharp knife, score the top 3 layers of pastry in your preferred shape of either squares or diamonds.

To finish, using a sharp knife trim the edges, or butter the untrimmed filo edges and fold them in to form a crust around the edge of the dish.

Bake in a moderate over for 45 minutes or until golden brown, and then remove from oven to cool.

Syrup

Place all ingredients into a small saucepan and heat over a stovetop. Stir until sugar is dissolved. Boil for 3 minutes and then add hot syrup over cooled pita.

If not using syrup, dust the pumpkin pita with sifted icing sugar before serving.

TIGANITES
FRIED DONUTS

Ingredients
2 cups self-raising flour
1 ½ cups warm water, from kettle
1 tablespoon light olive oil
3 tablespoons caster sugar
1 teaspoon pure vanilla essence
Sunflower oil, for deep-frying

Method
Sift the flour into a mixing bowl. In a glass bowl, place the water, olive oil, sugar, and vanilla essence. Mix well until sugar is dissolved. Make a well in the centre of the flour, and add the liquid. Mix thoroughly until smooth.

Place oil into a pot and heat gently over the stovetop. Place tablespoons of mixture into the hot oil, reduce heat slightly, and cook on one side for a few minutes, before turning over to cook the other side. Only turn once. When golden brown remove donuts and drain on absorbent paper.

To serve either sprinkle with caster sugar and ground cinnamon, or gently warm ½ cup of honey with 1 tablespoon of water to make a honey syrup.

Pour syrup over and dust with ground cinnamon.

PAXIMADIA
GREEK RUSKS

Ingredients
1 cup light flavoured olive oil
1 cup orange juice, freshly squeezed
1 cup caster sugar
2 ½ cups self-raising flour
2 ½ cups plain flour
1 teaspoon baking power
1 teaspoon ground aniseed or ground cinnamon
Sesame seeds (optional)

Method
Preheat oven to 180 degrees. Combine olive oil, orange juice and sugar and beat well. Place the remaining dry ingredients into a bowl and mix well.

Mix the wet ingredients into the dry ingredients and stir well using a wooden spoon. Knead the mixture to form a firm dough, and divide the mixture into 3 loaves about 5cm wide.

Transfer to a greased baking tray, and using a sharp knife cut the dough into 1cm widths. Brush the dough with a little water and sprinkle with sesame seeds. Bake at 180 degrees for 20 minutes or until golden brown.

Remove from oven. Using a knife separate the rusks, and rearrange the rusks laying them on their sides. Reduce oven temperature to 170 degrees. Bake for a further 20 minutes or until golden brown on all sides.

Cool on baking rack.

KOURAMBIEDES
Almond Shortbread

Ingredients
250 grams unsalted butter, at room temperature
2 tablespoons sunflower oil
2 tablespoons icing sugar, sifted
2 tablespoons caster sugar
1 egg yolk
1/2 cup blanched slivered almonds, toasted and chopped
3 cups self-raising flour
3 tablespoons Ouzo, Cognac or Mastiha
Icing Sugar

Method
Preheat the oven to 180 degrees. Place the butter, icing sugar and caster sugar into a large bowl, and beat together until the butter becomes pale and creamy, add egg yolk and liqueur of choice and mix well. Sift into the mixture the flour and add the toasted almonds. Use a wooden spoon to mix until well combined. Knead to bind the mixture together.

Take approximately 1 tablespoon of dough to form a ball, slightly roll into a log between the palms of your hands. Place onto baking tray, and slightly turn the ends to form a crescent. Pinch each end. Bake for 20 minutes until golden.

Remove from the oven and immediately allow the biscuits to cool on baking trays, before placing onto a sheet of baking paper that has been liberally dusted with loose icing sugar. Cover biscuits with more sifted icing sugar. Arrange on a serving plate, or store in a glass, airtight dish.

MELAMACARONA
HONEY WALNUT BISCUITS

Ingredients
1 1/2 cups sunflower oil
3/4 cup sugar
1 cup orange juice
1 cup fine semolina
5 cups self-raising flour, approximately
1 1/2 teaspoons baking soda
1 teaspoon ground nutmeg
2 teaspoons ground cinnamon
Zest of 1 orange
Crushed walnuts for decoration

Syrup
1 cup water
3/4 cup sugar
1/4 cup honey
1 cinnamon stick
3 whole clove buds
Thin slice of citrus rind

Method
Preheat the oven to 180 degrees. Beat together the oil, sugar, citrus zest and orange juice, before adding the spices, semolina and baking powder. Add the flour a little at a time, and gently knead to form a dough.

Take a walnut sized piece of dough, and form into oval shapes, pinching both ends to a blunt point.

MELAMACARONA
HONEY WALNUT BISCUITS (cont.)

Decorate the top of the biscuit with 5 diagonal lines using the tines of a fork, and bake for approximately 30 minutes or until the biscuits are firm and golden brown.

Syrup
Place all ingredients into a pot and bring to the boil, stirring constantly.

When completely cooled, dip 3-4 biscuits at a time into the hot syrup. Leave for 10 to 15 seconds.

Remove and then dip the top of each biscuit into the crushed walnuts.

Lift out onto a wire rack to cool.

* This recipe is suitable for vegans.

* Melamacarona can be stored in an airtight container in the fridge, that is if you can resist them.

PASTELLI
SEAME AND HONEY BARS

Ingredients
1 cup sesame seeds
1/2 cup honey
1/4 cup sugar
1 teaspoon vanilla sugar
1 teaspoon grated orange rind
1/2 cup almond slivers, toasted, for decoration

Method
Place the sesame seeds into a dry heavy based frying pan and toast gently. In another saucepan heat the honey until it begins to bubble, add the orange rind, sugar, and vanilla sugar. Stir well over low heat until sugar is dissolved, and transfer the toasted sesame seeds into the honey mixture and mix well. Continue boiling until a teaspoon of the mixture holds its shape when poured into a glass of cold water.

Place baking paper onto a glass board or marble slab, or other smooth surface. Working quickly, pour the mixture onto the baking paper, spread with a blunt knife, sprinkle with the toasted almond slivers, place another sheet of baking paper on top, and roll the mixture out thinly using a rolling pin.

Remove top layer of baking paper, and using a sharp knife proceed to cut into square or diamond shapes. Allow to cool.

Pastelli can be stored in an airtight container but you'll need to place a clean sheet of baking paper in between each layer, to prevent them from sticking together.

ROZEDES
SPICY ALMOND ROUNDS

Ingredients

4 cups blanched and finely ground almonds
½ cup caster sugar
½ cup breadcrumbs
½ cup fine semolina
1½ teaspoons ground cinnamon
1 teaspoon ground cloves
1 cup honey
½ cup water
Liqueur of your choice, Mastiha or Ouzo
Icing Sugar

Method

Preheat oven to 190 degrees. In a bowl, mix all ingredients except liqueur and icing sugar. Break off small pieces, the size of a walnut and form into round shapes.

Place onto a lined baking tray and using the back of a fork, flatten the mixture. Bake in a moderate oven for 20 minutes, and allow to cool slightly.

Brush the biscuits with the liqueur of your choice before dipping into a bowl of icing sugar and arranging the biscuits onto sheets of baking paper, sifting more icing sugar on top.

Leave overnight and then arrange onto your favourite serving plate.

Filo pastry is layer upon layer of wafer thin deliciousness that envelops a filling of choice, be it savoury or sweet.

FILO

HOME MADE FILO PASTRY

Ingredients
1 kg finely milled plain flour
2 cups warm water
1 teaspoon salt
½ cup olive oil or non-dairy butter (or non-dairy vegan spread)

Method
In a bowl combine the flour, salt, warm water and olive oil, and stir through to form a soft and elastic dough. If required, add a little more warm water. Knead the dough for approximately 10 minutes or until the pastry is smooth and round.

Divide the mixture into 12 equal portions, shaping them into balls. Cover with a clean cloth allowing dough to rest. Take one ball of dough at a time and flatten between the palms of your hands.

Place onto a lightly floured surface and using a rolling pin shape into 6-inch rounds. Brush with olive oil or non-dairy butter, and set aside.

Repeat this process for all 12 balls of dough, dividing them into two separate stacks of six rounds of dough. Do not brush the final layer of dough.

Lightly dust a large surface that can accommodate a long rolling pin or dowel, and dust the rolling pin with flour.

Place one stack of rounds onto the surface and begin rolling out as thin as possible. Repeat with the other stack of dough. Add a little flour if required to prevent sticking.

Place a clean tablecloth onto a flat surface and dust lightly with flour. Place the pastry onto the dowel and roll neatly turning the pastry back onto the dowel, and then continue to roll out. Repeat from opposite side, and exert gentle pressure to further stretch the pastry.

Place the back of your hands under the pastry and continue to move them gently towards the edges, creating an even thinner pastry. Finally the edges can be stretched using the fingertips.

Repeat this process with the remaining stack of dough.

Use one layer for the base of your pita, ensuring that there is pastry overhanging around the baking tray. Press down gently, and spoon the filling over the pastry and gently smooth out.

Place the other pastry layer on top, draping and folding as you go to create a 'gathered' look.

Using your fingers, bring the overhanging pastry up towards the top layer of pastry and turn and twist the edges tucking them inwards around the tray, to form a crust. Brush the top layer with a little more olive oil or non-dairy spread.

Using a sharp knife, lightly score the top layer of pastry into square or diamond shapes, and bake in a pre-heated moderate to hot oven for 45 minutes or until a deep golden brown.

THANK YOU

I do hope you enjoy the collation of my precious recipes that are authentic, sophisticated, uncomplicated and infused with sun-kissed ingredients and flavours that will tantalize your tastebuds.

I remain eternally grateful to my late mother Maria Desyllas for teaching me how to cook, and for the encouragement shown to me over the years. She imparted so many skills and know-how that have allowed me to also become an intuitive cook.

My father's culinary skills were just as amazing, and many times after my mother's passing he surprised us with home cooked meals.

I'd also like to thank my aunts, uncles, cousins and friends who have been so loving and welcoming since the time I met them as an eleven-year old in 1975 when I travelled to Greece with my father. Although some have sadly passed, the beautiful people that remain continue to open their hearts and warmly welcome me into their lives, seamlessly picking up from where we left off from previous visits.

Last but not least, thank you dear reader, for adding my latest book to your collection. I hope this cookbook will be enjoyed for years to come.

With love, Eugenia x

PHOTOGRAPHY

The photos within Greek Food For Sharing are my own with the exception of those taken by Zoe Coates, with author's own props, as follows:

Grecian decor, page 37
Tarama, page 38
Beetroot, page 126
Ouzo, pages 46 and 119
Coffee, page 142
Melamacarona page 147 and 160
Selected food and table settings were photographed at the homes of relatives and friends as follows:

My cousin, Eugenia Zisogiannopoulou
Fassolada page 66
Fassolakia, page 92
Liqueur, page 163

My cousin, Constantina Zisogiannopoulou
Fakes Soup and Red Peppers, page 51
Cod Stew, page 83
Fish, Red Peppers and Salad, page 97

My friend, Asimo Tzoniki
Fried Fish and mezedes, page 82
Kitchen, page 91

My Aunt Dimitra Mastorelli
Coffee and Spoon Sweets on tray, page 142

My late father John Desyllas
Spaghetti with Meat Sauce, page 118
Photographed at his home.

INDEX

Arni Psisto – Roast Lamb	81
Arni Yahni – Braised Lamb	78
Avgolemono – Chicken Egg Lemon Soup	63
Bakaliaros Yahni - Cod Stew	85
Boughatsa – Baked Pastry with Custard	150
Briami – Baked Vegetables	101
Brocollo – Brocolli Salad	122
Dolmades – Stuffed Vine Leaves	47
Fakes – Lentil Soup	69
Fassolada – White Bean Soup	67
Fassolakia me Patates – Green Bean and Potato Stew	93
Fassolia – Green Bean Salad	123
Filo Pastry	171
Fish, Fried	83
Fish, Baked	90
Frappe – Iced Coffee	146
Fruit	138
Garides Saganaki – Prawns in Tomato Sauce	53
Greek Coffee	145
Horiatiki Salata – Greek Salad	131
Horta – Boiled Greens	129
Kalamari Kokkinisto – Braised Calamari	88
Kalamari Tiganito – Fried Calamari	49
Karidi Skordalia – Walnut Dip	36
Keftedes - Meatballs	58
Kolokithakia Tiganita – Fried Zuchinni	55
Kolokithopita – Pumpkin Pie	153
Kotopouloa Kokkinisto - Braised Chicken	79
Kourambiedes – Almond Shortbread	159
Kounoupidi Salata – Cauliflower Salad	124
Kounoupidi Yahni – Braised Cauliflower	106

Macaronia me Kima – Macaroni with Mince Sauce 117
Macaronia me Tiri – Macaroni with Cheese.................................. 115
Macaronia me Tomata Salsa – Pasta with Tomato Salsa 113
Manestra – Risoni Soup.. 71
Manitaria Soup – Mushroom Soup.. 75
Marouli Salata – Lettuce Salad.. 133
Mapa Salata - Greek Coleslaw.. 135
Melamacarona – Honey Walnut Biscuits 161
Melizana sti Skara – Grilled Eggplant 50
Melizanes Ladera – Baked Eggplant 104
Melizanosalata – Aubergine Dip 34
Moussaka – Aubergine with Meat Sauce 98

Pantzaria – Beetroot Salad 127
Pastelli – Sesame Honey Bars 165
Pastitsio – Macaroni and Meat Pie... 94
Patata Salata – Potato Salad 125
Patates Yahni – Braised Potatoes 107
Paximadia - Greek Rusks 157
Pita Bread – Grilled Pita Bread... 43
Psari Plaki – Baked Fish.. 90
Psari Tiganito – Fried Fish.. 83

Revithia Yahni – Braised Chickpeas 117
Rizi me Kanella – Cinnamon Rice... 110
Rozedes – Spicy Almond Rounds... 167

Skordalia – Garlic Dip 35
Spanakopita – Spinach Pie.. 57
Spanakorizo – Spinach with Rice.. 109

Taramasalata – Caviar Dip 39
Tiganites – Fried Donuts 155
Tomato Soupa – Tomato Soup with Pasta 72
Tyrokafteri – Spicy Feta Dip.. 42
Tzatziki Yoghurt Cucumber Dip... 41

White Bean Dip 33

Yemista – Rice Stuffed Vegetables... 102

www.ingramcontent.com/pod-product-compliance
Lightning Source LLC
Chambersburg PA
CBHW042056290426
44112CB00001B/5